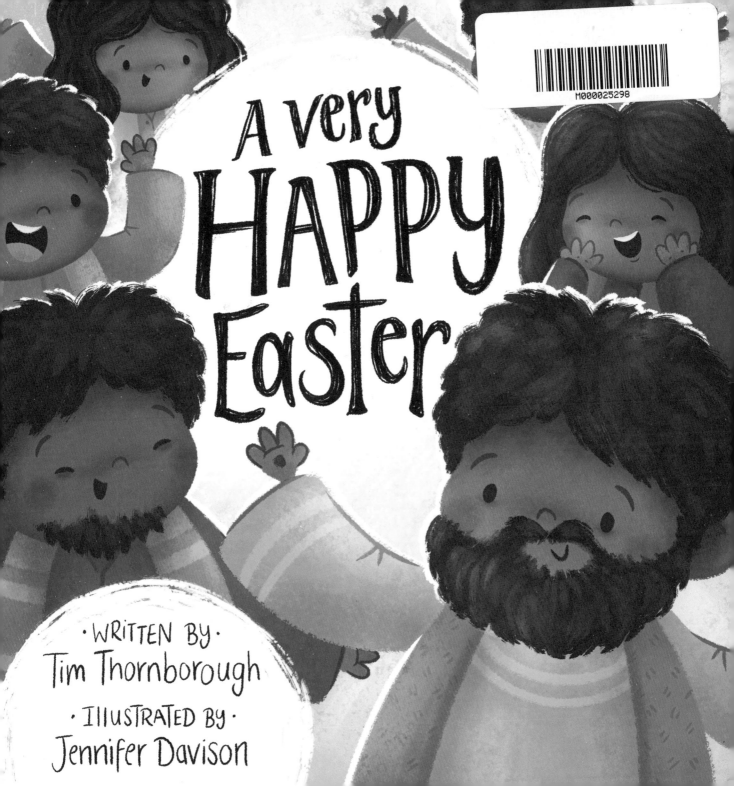

A very HAPPY Easter

· WRITTEN BY ·
Tim Thornborough

· ILLUSTRATED BY ·
Jennifer Davison

A Very Happy Easter © The Good Book Company, 2019

Words by Tim Thornborough. Illustrations by Jennifer Davison. Design and art direction by André Parker

UK: www.thegoodbook.co.uk North America: www.thegoodbook.com Australia: www.thegoodbook.com.au

ISBN: 9781784983666. Printed in India

This book is a bit different from others.

In most books there is work for your eyes and ears.
You look at the pictures, and listen to the words.

But in this book, there is work for your face too!

You will see the faces of lots of people who were there at
the first Easter when Jesus died and rose again.

Every time you see one, try to copy the face they are making,
and think about how they would have felt...

Let's try it!

Are you ready?

Then turn the page to begin...

Jesus came to the city of Jerusalem.

A huge **EXCITED** crowd welcomed Jesus.
They knew that he was God's promised King.

But some people did not want Jesus to be in charge.

So they sent soldiers to arrest him. They **HATED** Jesus, because he said he was the Son of God.

They put King Jesus on a cross to die.
Jesus' friends were very SCARED.

Jesus died.
His friends CRIED.

They buried Jesus in a rock tomb
and put a big heavy

STONE
over the
DOOR.

Jesus' friends were so so SAD.

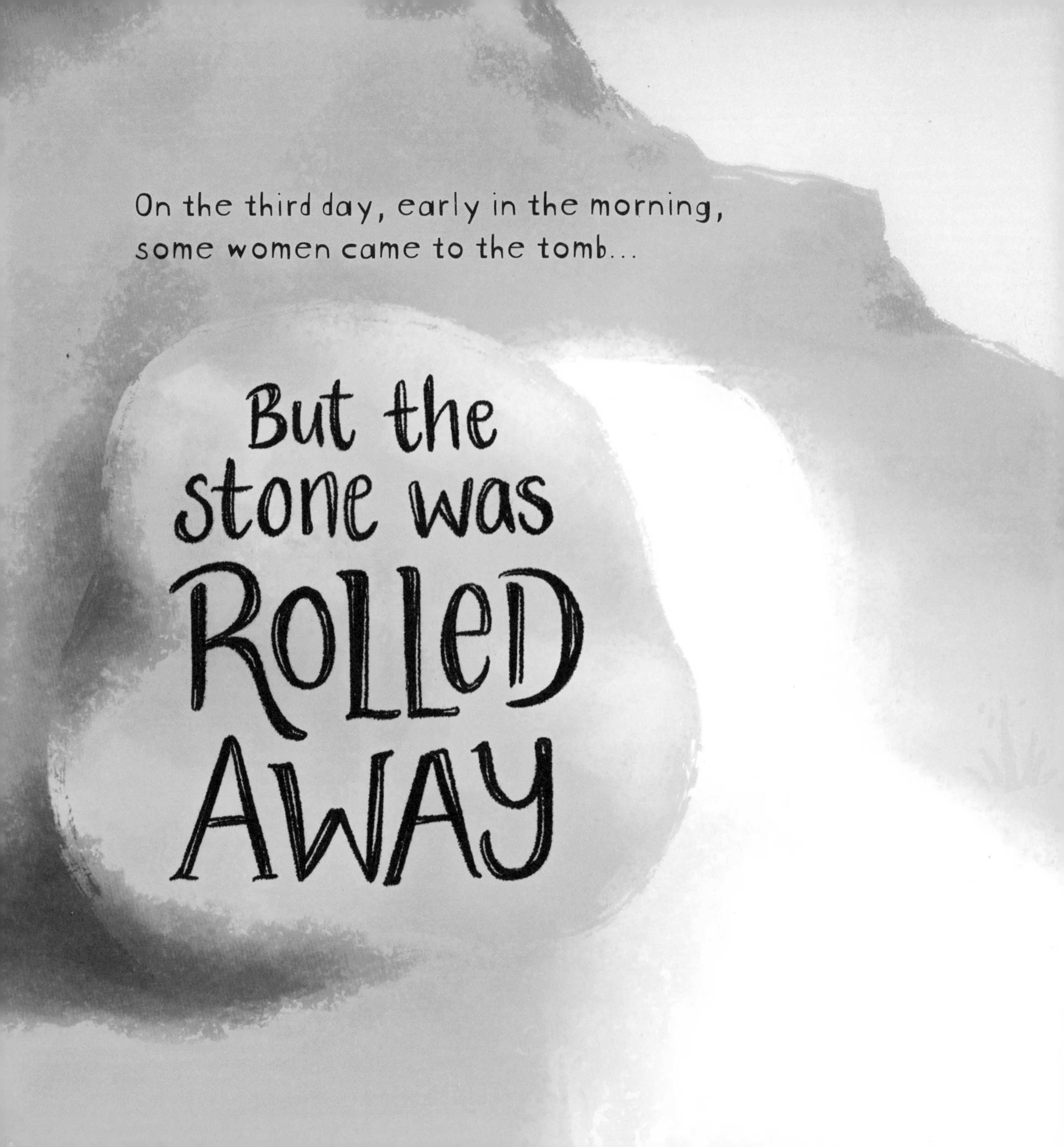

On the third day, early in the morning,
some women came to the tomb...

But the
stone was
ROLLED
AWAY

Jesus was not there!
They were so so CONFUSED...

Some angels appeared.
They said:

"He is
NOT
HERE".

"HE IS
RISen!"

...Just as he promised.

The women were
ASTONISHED!

The women ran and told Jesus' friends what they had seen and what the angels had said.

"HE is Risen!"

But they **DIDN'T BELIEVE** them...

Suddenly, Jesus was right there with them.

He
SPOKE
to them

He
ATE
with
them

He
SHOWED
them His
HANDS
AND FEET

He really was
alive again!

"Don't be afraid", said Jesus. "It really is me!"

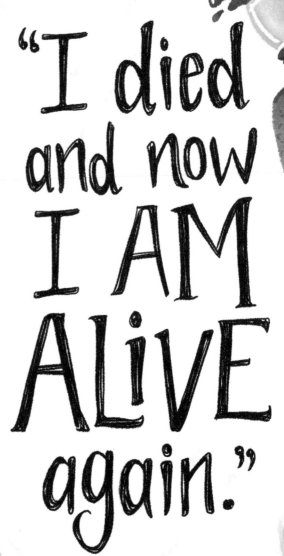

"I died and now I AM ALiVE again."

Now you can be friends with God forever!

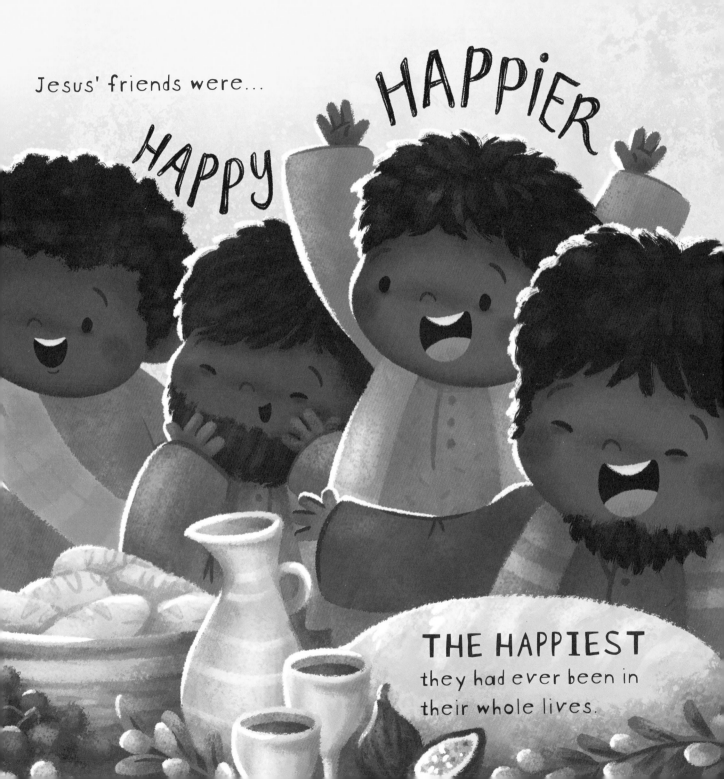

Jesus' friends were...

HAPPY

HAPPIER

THE HAPPIEST
they had ever been in
their whole lives.

Then King Jesus sent his friends to tell everyone the Good News.

They HAPPILY spread the message all over the world.

And now YOU have heard the message about how King Jesus died and rose again so that we can be friends with God forever.